The Evergreen School
15201 Meridian Ave. N
Shoreline, WA 98133

ALL AROUND THE WORLD
SWITZERLAND

by Kristine Spanier

Ideas for Parents and Teachers

Pogo Books let children practice reading informational text while introducing them to nonfiction features such as headings, labels, sidebars, maps, and diagrams, as well as a table of contents, glossary, and index.

Carefully leveled text with a strong photo match offers early fluent readers the support they need to succeed.

Before Reading

- "Walk" through the book and point out the various nonfiction features. Ask the student what purpose each feature serves.
- Look at the glossary together. Read and discuss the words.

Read the Book

- Have the child read the book independently.
- Invite him or her to list questions that arise from reading.

After Reading

- Discuss the child's questions. Talk about how he or she might find answers to those questions.
- Prompt the child to think more. Ask: The mountains of Switzerland are well known. What natural landforms are well known where you live?

Pogo Books are published by Jump!
5357 Penn Avenue South
Minneapolis, MN 55419
www.jumplibrary.com

Library of Congress Cataloging-in-Publication Data

Names: Spanier, Kristine, author.
Title: Switzerland / by Kristine Spanier.
Description: Minneapolis, MN : Jump, Inc., 2020.
"Pogo Books are published by Jump!"
Includes bibliographical references and index.
Identifiers: LCCN 2018048625 (print)
LCCN 2018049921 (ebook)
ISBN 9781641286640 (ebook)
ISBN 9781641286626 (hardcover : alk. paper)
ISBN 9781641286633 (pbk.)
Subjects: LCSH: Switzerland–Juvenile literature.
Classification: LCC DQ17 (ebook)
LCC DQ17 .S67 2020 (print) | DDC 949.4–dc23
LC record available at https://lccn.loc.gov/2018048625

Editor: Susanne Bushman
Designer: Leah Sanders

Photo Credits: Jakl Lubos/Shutterstock, cover; PatrickHutter/Getty, 1; Pixfiction/Shutterstock, 3; Koray Bektas/Shutterstock, 4; Vaclav Volrab/Shutterstock, 5; Marcin Perkowski/Shutterstock, 6t; Simon Weber Santos/Shutterstock, 6b; Ondrej Prosicky/Shutterstock, 6-7t; robysbenzi/iStock, 6-7b; sorincolac/iStock, 8; Fedor Selivanov/Shutterstock, 9; imageBROKER/Superstock, 10-11; AMELIE-BENOIST/BSIP/Superstock, 12-13; FABRICE COFFRINI/AFP/Getty, 14-15; Westend61/Superstock, 16; gorillaimages/Shutterstock, 17; Denis Linine/Shutterstock, 18-19; NicolasMcComber/iStock, 20-21; mkos83/Shutterstock, 23.

Printed in the United States of America at Corporate Graphics in North Mankato, Minnesota.

TABLE OF CONTENTS

CHAPTER 1

WELCOME TO SWITZERLAND!

Taste fondue. Listen to a
yodeler. Take a train trip
from Zermatt to St. Moritz
on the Glacier Express.
You will cross 291 bridges.
And go through 91 tunnels!
Welcome to Switzerland!

tunnel

Glacier
Express

Matterhorn

This country is **landlocked**. The Jura Mountains border the north and west. The Alps span the southeast. Matterhorn is a peak in the Alps. It looks like a pyramid. It is 14,692 feet (4,478 meters) high!

fox

badger

marmot

ibex

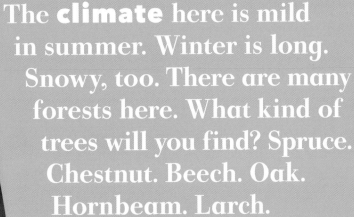

The **climate** here is mild in summer. Winter is long. Snowy, too. There are many forests here. What kind of trees will you find? Spruce. Chestnut. Beech. Oak. Hornbeam. Larch.

The forests make good homes for foxes. Badgers. Squirrels. Marmots and chamois live in the Alps. Herds of ibex, too.

CHAPTER 2

SWISS PEOPLE

More than half of Swiss people live in apartments. Most are in cities like Zürich. It is the largest city here. People enjoy boating in Lake Zürich.

Zürich

Chalets are popular homes. Where? In mountain villages. In winter, you will see people ice-skating. Skiing. And going for **toboggan** rides!

chalet

The country is divided into 26 cantons. These are like states. The Federal Assembly meets in Bern, the **capital**. People vote for its members. These members make laws.

The Federal Council leads the government. A new member is **president** each year.

DID YOU KNOW?

The Swiss have a history of staying **neutral**. When? During two big wars. World War I (1914–1918). And World War II (1939–1945). It has not been in a war since 1815.

What languages are spoken here? German. French. Italian. And Romansh. Every canton chooses one. Students study this language in school. They work on math and science, too. They must go to school until they are at least 15 years old. Most finish upper secondary school. They learn skills for jobs there. Some go on to university, or college.

WHAT DO YOU THINK?

Good **boarding schools** are here. Students live and study at them. They come from around the world. Would you like to go to school away from home?

Many people work in **manufacturing**. The Swiss are known for their watches and clocks. They also make motors and wind turbines. Banking is another important job.

Swiss watch

CHAPTER 3

FOOD, FUN, AND CELEBRATIONS

Ice hockey is a popular sport here. Soccer, too. And Schwingen, or Swiss wrestling. The Swiss love to ski or climb the mountains.

fondue ·····▶

Try fondue! It is a pot of melted cheese. You dip bread into it. Raclette is also good. It is cheese melted over a fire. People often put it on potatoes.

Yodeling is a **tradition** here. Swiss people do it at town festivals. Alphorn blowing, too. This was once a way to **communicate** from one **pasture** to another. Some alphorns are 12 feet (3.7 m) long!

alphorn

TAKE A LOOK!

• •

Traditional outfits are worn at festivals. Each canton has its own. But many share similar **elements**.

BONNET

FELT HAT

VEST

CORSET

TROUSERS

APRON

SKIRT

SHOES

Dorffest marks the end of summer. People go to concerts. They dance and sing. Cattle come down from mountain pastures. People wrap bulls' horns with flowers. They put large bells around their necks.

This is a beautiful country. Would you like to visit?

WHAT DO YOU THINK?

August 1 is National Day. People picnic. They watch fireworks. Do you have a day to celebrate the country where you live?

bell

QUICK FACTS & TOOLS

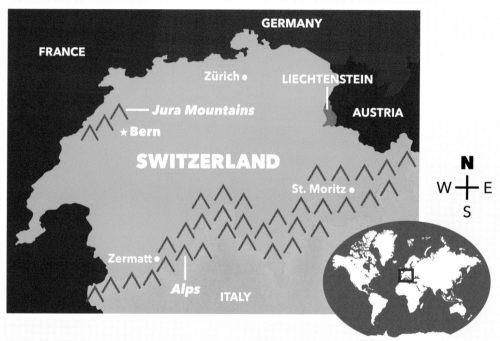

SWITZERLAND

Location: central Europe

Size: 15,937 square miles
(41,277 square kilometers)

Population: 8,292,809
(July 2018 estimate)

Capital: Bern

Type of Government:
federal republic

Languages: German, French,
Italian, Romansh

Exports: machinery, watches,
agricultural products

Currency: Swiss franc

GLOSSARY

boarding schools: Schools where students reside during the school term.

capital: A city where government leaders meet.

climate: The weather typical of a certain place over a long period of time.

communicate: To share information with others.

elements: The simple, basic parts of something.

landlocked: Not having any borders that touch the sea.

manufacturing: The industry of making something on a large scale using special equipment or machinery.

neutral: Not supporting or agreeing with either side of a disagreement.

pasture: Grazing land for animals.

president: The leader of a country, sometimes in a ceremonial position.

toboggan: A long, narrow sled used to coast downhill.

tradition: A custom, belief, or activity that is handed down from one generation to the next.

yodeling: Singing loudly in a voice that changes quickly between high and low sounds.

Switzerland's currency

INDEX

TO LEARN MORE

Finding more information is as easy as 1, 2, 3.

1. Go to www.factsurfer.com
2. Enter "Switzerland" into the search box.
3. Click the "Surf" button to see a list of websites.

FACT SURFER